2.1 JOBS.. WORK..

EMPLOYMENT.. CAREERS

THE HIDDEN SECRETS

Eddie Powell

Leading Authority on Workforce and

Business Development

Eddie@EddiePowell.com

Proven Method Of Success

JOBS.. WORK..

EMPLOYMENT.. CAREERS

THE HIDDEN SECRETS

By: Eddie Powell

Leading Authority on Workforce and Business

Development

Eddie@EddiePowell.com

www.EddiePowell.com

Let's Connect On: Facebook, LinkedIn, and

Others!

What used to be is no longer it seems in the realm of employment, careers, the world of work, and jobs. In your grandparents day it was typical to find a job in a factory, go to work there for 20 years, get your gold watch at your retirement party, then live happily for the rest of your life on your pension and social security payments. That's the way it worked and many people chose this option. Those that did not chose this avenue, usually ran their own business, tried to save some money for retirement, and happily operated their automotive repair shop, plumbing, remodeling, tv repair shop, or local retail store. Oh sure, there were some teaching, preaching, fighting fires or criminals, patching up the broken bones, and working for small town governments patching the streets or delivering the mail, but these were the support team members of the factory working crowd. Each did their duty and days went by…

Somewhere between then and now, there was a huge shift in the workforce and how work is done. For some it was abrupt, for others the technology and change snuck in the side door. But, each soon realized that the world that they had been working in, the dreams they had been building were gone, replaced by new rules, new idea's, new people with a whole variety of new expectations. Knocked off balance with their heads still spinning the Baby Boomers have come to realize that they need to upgrade, get online, and become more efficient. Gen X and Gen Y have come roaring in with their degrees and technology to begin to rewrite the future they were not asked to be a part of nor able to accept.

As if these demographic shifts in the numbers, volume, and experience of workers is not enough, the workers of the world have come knocking at the door. They have brought with them different experiences, cultures, traditions, value expressions, and governments full of regulations and expectations. Some want the machining, others want to build the cars, still others want the textiles, and more want to tout their technology. It seems for every niche there are numerous countries packed with workers that want to get their share of the world economic pie. They present their offerings of better quality, less expensive workforce, logistics, and other determined advantages to businesses focused on quarterly bottomline profits as opportunities while challenging the former status quo, dismantling dreams and lifestyles along the way only to be replaced by different names and faces with different dreams.

Add to all these changes, a world without walls, in which businesses from nearly any country operate and sell in nearly any other market in the world. Gen X and Gen Y workers in the USA provide less workers than the huge number of Baby Boomers that are marching toward retirement and exit from the workforce. South American countries are experiencing positive population growth while Europe and elsewhere around the world are experiencing a negative population growth, meaning there are fewer potential workers being born than current exist in the area. Educated workers in Egypt and other countries want their shot at success yet are stifled with not enough opportunity to work. The Asian Rim including China provides a huge population of workers that want to improve their standard of living for their families, same in India and elsewhere. Yet, countries that seemingly refuse to leave their old way are being pushed to the position of least successful in the world.

Changes In Work, Careers, & Employment

Demographic shifts change things. The worker becomes the retiree. The family needing the big house becomes the family with children moving out and downsizing in their future. Similar, too, are the lifestyle changes in healthcare, transportation, travel, second homes in other climates, food, recreation, clothing, buying for grandchildren, and more.

Couple the above mentioned items with technology changes, automation, immigration, changes in governments, currencies, religious influences, climate changes, natural and man-made disasters, and so many other world pressures affecting the status of work, careers, and employment. Moves from "E Commerce" to "M Commerce" (mobile commerce), from brick-and-mortar to commerce without countries or walls, cloud computing, employing alternative workforce segments, automating such repetitive tasks as fast-food ordering or political campaign calls, and much more.

These changes also bring new opportunities. For instance, social media marketing manager is a hot new career that expands on the commerce without walls idea and connects Facebook, Twitter, App's, SMS, and YouTubes with products and offerings. Housing foreclosures bring opportunities for rehab construction teams versus construction companies focused on new builds. Mechanics see more long-term use of existing cars versus new car purchases during a down economy. Home improvement stores help with repairs, grocery is challenged with rising prices, thus, less food or lower priced food becomes more popular than eating out during down times. The same is true in many niche categories as opportunities can only be seen after changes in perception.

Holding on to the past mindset sees all of this as the dying of the dinosaur and those that cannot change their mindset will struggle with trying to save their cultural icon(s). Those that embrace change see all of this as a race to the future to grab their share with the new weapons of technology, global competition actually being global partnership and opportunity, along with the actual displays of innovation and design as the stepping stones to success!

What is going on in the Job Market?

Today's job market is quite exciting, volatile, and seems to expand or contract with the mere whisper of a few words at the stock market or at the Federal Reserve with regard to interest rates, how robust the economy is, and how many jobs are being moved overseas. All of this changes moment to moment, it seems. But, should *you* worry?

In nearly every economy of the past 30 years there have been ways to get jobs and work to be had for those that were willing to search it out and think a little outside the norms. Is this still true today?

I say "yes"! Yes, for those that walk the walk and talk the talk! Yes, for those that really sell themselves! Yes, for those that network! Yes, for those with a resume that sizzles! Yes, for those that check both the front door and the back door! Yes, for you... no matter if you are just out of school, wanting to change jobs or careers, or feeling like the ugly duckling that will never be accepted!

If you will read and follow my instructions in this book, you will realize a positive outlook that you may have never had, learn the secrets to interviewing, know what the employers are searching for, and be more able to "sell yourself" in a way that may have seemed impossible to you prior to reading and applying this information.

Everybody's got a "dream job" that they have longed for, a job that they would just love to have and do for a long, long time. Well, now is the moment that you've been waiting for - the time to change your life and go after all it is that you've only been dreaming about!

Ready??

Well, let's go... and literally

CHANGE *YOUR* LIFE!

-

The Job Market for some creates fear, intimidation, and raises up a whole host of emotions that many times are hard to deal with. Some of these feelings are brought about by the stories we've heard from well-meaning friends and relatives or from former employees of a particular company that may have had a stressful experience, as they seek to pass on exaggerated information.

The Job Market can be very intimidating for people that do not do their homework prior to entering. Sometimes it's the thought of having to interview with someone that knows nothing about me and having to "sell" myself to them. Most of us would say, "I'm not a sales person. How do you expect me to "sell" myself when I've never sold anything before and I sure don't want to start now!?"

Others get emotional over the information that they should include in their resume. This is all very personal stuff, true. "What if I get rejected?" you ask. I'll talk about that in an upcoming chapter.

Hopefully, as you read, think about, and apply the information, suggestions, and idea's that I have compiled in this book, you will gain greater insight into yourself, your purpose in life, and the type of work that you would like to be doing... you know, the work that would really make you happy.

After all, isn't that what life is all about? Living, loving, laughing, and doing that which makes us happy. Why should your job, your work, your career choice be anything less?

Truth is, it isn't all about money or prestige, or power, or position, or doing some job that made your mom, dad, or spouse happy... it's about being happy, really happy, deep down inside within your heart of hearts!

If you can come to realize this and know how to apply this wisdom to your career choice, your life will take on new meaning, priorities will change, and your life will take on new purpose and direction!

With this in mind, the direction of the stock market, the openness or tightness of the job market, or even what others will say and have you believe are not important, for you are the one and only you - you have worth, you are valuable, and you have creative idea's!

Certainly, no one has the corner on the knowledge market, and thus, you are equal, valuable, and as capable of receiving and giving back to the universe as anyone else is.

Pay no attention to the nay sayers for they seek to diminish your dreams and desires but instead, listen to your heart, your dreams, your desires and realize that you are being lead to realize your purpose in life!

Know that it is not a job that you want but a fulfillment of purpose in your life!

Therefore, the circumstances around you will change as you become in tune with and begin reaching for your own personal vision of fulfillment.

I once saw an interview with an Olympic runner. When asked about the race and how it felt to win, she stated that it all felt very comfortable. When asked to expand on that thought, she replied, "I had envisioned myself winning in my minds eye. I saw myself winning, crossing that finish line first. From there I just backed through the race in my head, back to the starting point. Then, when the gun sounded and the race began, it was all very comfortable to me. I just did it as I had envisioned it."

The same can be true of accomplishing your life's work, your purpose. The race... *your race*... will be run and won in your mind, first!

You must get out of that mindset of needing and begging for a job! Never again will you "beg for a job"!

Start right now thinking of yourself as a Free Agent, just like the ball players. What do they do? They shop their talents to various ball clubs, invite offers, and accept the offer that they choose for themselves.

Do they accept what is presented? No way, they negotiate! If the ball club offered 3 million and a Volkswagen perhaps they counter with 10 million and a Jag. After some negotiation, they come to an agreement that they both can live with and sign on the dotted line.

The same is true with you! You have certain talents that you can shop to various employers. You can invite offers. You can counteroffer. Then you can accept the one that is the best for you, the one that you can live with, the one that allows you to grow towards that purpose for your life!

Who me negotiate?

Why not? If they offer $20,000 a year with 2 weeks vacation and medical benefits perhaps you may chose to counter with $28,000 a year 3 weeks vacation, medical, dental, vision, and tuition benefits.

Somewhere in between should be your compromise point, the point at which you both could live and be happy. They get a happy employee living out their dream at a price they can afford and you get the opportunity to work in the field that gives your life meaning and purpose while maintaining a lifestyle that well suits you.

Can this happen or is this just some more dreaming?

Ah, the answer is totally up to you! What is it that would bring you to a sense of being on purpose? What other information do you need to know and practice prior to setting forth to live your dream? Do you really know your self?

Let's go forward and find out.

KNOW YOURSELF

(AND THE JOB YOU WOULD ENJOY)

Who are you? Really, who are you? Let's do an exercise right now that will help you discover more about yourself and who you are.

Simply take a sheet of paper and number from one to thirty five going down the left hand side. Now, next to each number, list a talent that you are good at.

You may choose talents like: I am a good housekeeper; I like to organize; I like to plant flowers; I enjoy music trivia; I like to travel; and so forth.

Do it now and don't stop until you have 35.

1.

2.

3.

4.

5.

6.

7.

8.

9.

10.

11.

12.

13.

14.

15.

16.

17.

18.

19.

20.

21.

22.

23.

24.

25.

26.

27.

28.

29.

30.

31.

32.

33.

34.

35.

List more if you wish.

Now that you have 35 talents, things that you enjoy doing. Look over your list and choose 3 things that you enjoy doing the most in life.

Just 3, like: I enjoy movies; I like planting flowers; and I like being a friend.

Choose wisely but remember, if you wish you may go back later and choose 3 different ones.

Write them down...

1.

2.

3.

Now, carefully look them over and see if there is a
way that you could combine two or three of them into
an occupation, a life purpose, that could generate
some revenue for you.

For instance, I like being a friend and I like planting flowers could combine to allow for a life purpose of planting flowers and growing flowers for older folks that can no longer plant flower beds and get down on their knees but yet would welcome a loving, caring person like you to come to their home and care for their flowers for them for a fee.

Could this be your purpose? Would this make you happy? Do you know anyone that could help you on this life journey?

Now, go back to your list. Are there any combinations that you can create or realize for yourself that would put you on purpose and allow you to be happy with your life while generating an income for you? Could this be something that you would like to pursue or do you need to go back to your list and choose again? You may repeat this exercise as many times as you need to discover yourself and what would really make you happy!

Take your time, think it through, and seek to know your own heart. I believe you will pleasantly surprised. I will be waiting up ahead.

Selling Yourself

If you are like most people you panic when the word "sell" is included in any sentence that also includes "you". You may say that you know nothing about selling, let alone selling yourself. You might also insist that you have never sold anything before in your life and that you are not about to start now.

Well, let me ask you, "Do you have any friends?"
"Have you ever sold an old car you used to have?"
"Have you ever convinced the teacher that your dog
ate your homework?"

You were selling!

You were selling yourself to new friends, an object to
a person that wanted to buy your old car, and your
personal story to the teacher. You were selling then
and you are selling yourself everyday... to your co-
workers, friends, even the police officer that stopped
you that you tried to convince otherwise about that
traffic ticket!

Selling is not some dirty word nor is it really all that tough, once you know a few secrets that I am about to share with you.

First, let me put you in the mindset of a marketer. If you, as a marketer, were seeking to sell automobiles what would you do first? Take a look at your product and compare it to the competition. Notice anything similar? Well, they both have steering wheels, seats, windows, a muffler, and four wheels on the ground, among other things.

Now, think about all the car commercials for the different makes and models of cars... are any of them selling the steering wheel, the tires, the muffler, etc.? No. These are features. Instead, the car companies are selling benefits. Benefits like this is the fastest, this one takes you to the mountains, this one allows you to cut in and out of traffic, this is the newest, bluest, best gas mileage, etc. Benefits… all benefits!

OK, now you are your own marketer for your own product - "***PRODUCT YOU***!"

Compare your product to the competition. They both have a resume, some education, some work history, some experience, etc. Think like a marketer and tell me your benefits…

…benefits like "I can lead, direct, and manage…" "I can implement, upgrade, and increase production by 110%…" "I can interact with new suppliers and establish previously undiscovered clients to save on hard costs while creating entirely new markets…"

Now, write down no more than three sentences that describe your benefits from a marketers perspective.

Remember, you are selling _PRODUCT YOU_.

I am including an extensive list of action verbs I call POWERVERBS. These are words that convey action, focus, and a sense of purpose. Obviously, these are not the only words in the English language that relay this sense of purpose, but these are representative. You may certainly choose to incorporate some of your own.

POWERVERBS

| Accelerated | Coordinated | Helped |

Provided	Accomplished	Counseled
Hired	Published	Achieved
Created	Identified	Raised
Acquainted	Decreased	Illustrated
Reconciled		
Adapted	Delegated	Implemented
Recorded		
Administered	Demonstrated	Improved
Recruited		
Advised	Designed	Increased
Reduced		
Aided	Detected	Informed
Regulated		
Allocated	Determined	Initiated
Reorganized		

Analyzed	Developed	Innovated
Reported		
Answered	Devised	Inspired
Represented		
Appointed	Directed	Installed
Researched	Apprised	Discovered
Instilled	Resolved	Arbitrated
Disseminated	Instituted	Responded
Arranged	Dissuaded	Instituted
Restored	Assembled	Distributed
Instructed	Restructured	Assisted
Documented	Integrated	Retrieved
Attained	Drafted	Interpreted
Revamped	Attended	Edited

Interviewed	Reviewed	Audited
Educated	Introduced	Revised
Augmented	Elected	Invented
Revitalized	Authored	Eliminated
Launched	Revolutionized	
Awarded	Encouraged	Lectured
Routed	Balanced	Enforced
Led	Saved	Boosted
Enlisted	Listened	Scheduled
Briefed	Ensured	Maintained
Searched	Broadened	Established
Managed	Secured	Budgeted
Evaluated	Marketed	Selected
Built	Examined	Mastered

Settled	Calculated	Exceeded
Mediated	Shaped	Cataloged
Excelled	Mentored	Sold
Catered	Executed	Moderated
Solicited	Centralized	Expanded
Modernized	Solved	Chaired
Expedited	Monitored	Spearheaded
Collaborated	Explained	Motivated
Spoke	Collected	Extracted
Negotiated	Sponsored	Comforted
Fabricated	Operated	Staged
Compiled	Facilitated	Organized
Started	Composed	Familiarized
Originated	Streamlined	Computed

Financed	Oversaw	Strengthened
Conceived	Formalized	Performed
Summarized	Conceptualized	Formed
Persuaded	Supervised	Conducted
Formulated	Pioneered	Supplemented
Constructed	Fostered	Planned
Supported	Consulted	Founded
Prepared	Surveyed	Contacted
Gained	Presented	Taught
Contributed	Gathered	Presided
Trained	Convinced	Guided
Processed	Wrote	Worked

(Remember, this is not a dictionary… can you think of more PowerVerbs?)

Rewrite. Use some of these in your sentences. Create more sentences.

Think like a marketer selling _PRODUCT YOU_... again, give me the benefits!

Complete the following sentence:

**"I can benefit your organization by _powerverb_,
powerverb, and _powerverb_ for _benefit or result_."**

See how easy it is to sell yourself?

You should seek to incorporate several of these POWERVERBS into your vocabulary. You should have two, three, or more of these types of sentences memorized so that in any setting, if you are ever asked, you can sell yourself without question and without hesitation! Write a dozen, then memorize the best.

1.

2.

3.

4.

5.

Establishing Your Network

Establishing your network is something that you have been working on all your life, yet you may not have realized it. Your network is a collection of family, friends, business acquaintances, and other people that you encounter on your journey through life.

For instance, your Pastor, the parents at your child's scout meetings, golfing buddies, and folks that you volunteer with at your favorite charity are all people that you have encountered in your life that may provide you with valuable leads and information on jobs and career opportunities that you may be interested in.

The purpose of establishing a network of people is that they can serve as your eyes and ears as you search for your next career opportunity.

Wouldn't it be nice if friends and contacts were calling you to inform you of opportunities and to see if you would be interested in working with them? Imagine the legwork you'd save and the quality of information that you would be receiving, all without reading a single want ad in the newspaper.

But, the question remains, how do I establish just such a network?

Obviously, you can discuss with friends and family that you are always looking for career opportunities and advancement in your chosen career field.

Acquaintances may be a little more difficult to talk about your career search with but if you call them with something that you have heard about that they may be interested in, thus, giving to them first, you will approach the subject in the most winning of ways possible.

You can further increase your network and, therefore, the quantity and quality of your potential leads by expanding the number of people within your network. This can be accomplished by calling a company that you would consider working for and asking for the supervisor of the department you would consider working in and ask them for a few minutes of their time at a time convenient for them.

Let's say you agree on Tuesday at 3:00pm to talk over the phone. Be committed to your word and call at the agreed upon time to discuss all you'd like to know about your proposed career choice from the expert, as you have prearranged.

During the discussion, you may choose to bring up questions related to career opportunities both at their company and others within the industry. Explore that line of questioning in a polite and tactful way so as to allow the expert to remain non-committed yet establish them as a contact that could feel free to contact you, should they become aware of something specific that may fit your particular talents, skills, and qualifications.

You have successfully added this expert to your own network, informed them about you and your career search, and gathered quality information while recognizing them for their knowledge, position, and access to information that could be valuable to you.

In other words, you have appealed to their ego while asking for their help. This is a strategy that may pay huge dividends in the future.

This same backdoor type of information gathering may be applied to companies, authors, career counselors, chamber of commerce's, networking groups, and others.

Remember, your goal in this method is not landing a job immediately but in obtaining some quality lead information and informing your new network expert of your qualifications and career search within the industry. Those leads may generate the career position that you are ideally searching for.

Networking is something that you should be doing consistently for the rest of your life.

Bear in mind that most people will change careers - not just jobs but entire career focus - six to eight times in their lifetime.

Your network can assist you with career advancement and career changes, so stay in contact with your team.

Contact, cultivate, and continue building your network... starting now!

Walking the Walk and Talking the Talk

Ever stopped to consider what the difference is between you and everyone else that walked through the door wanting that same career position that you want?

Your answer should include the benefits you bring to the table as stated with several powerverbs in your sentences and your personal commitment. Commitment, now there's a word that many people use in the career search process but few can actually illustrate it.

Let's look at commitment like this:

Say you walk over to the nearest wall, with feet flat on the floor, and raise your hand above your head to mark the highest point on the wall you can reach - Mark it.

Now, same wall, same arm, stretch, really stretch, stand on your tip toes, and reach as high as you possibly can - Mark it.

Notice the difference between the two marks.

The first mark represents everyone that walked through that door, suited up, and ready to play. This is the long list of potential candidates for any job.

The second mark represents that 10% better than everyone else you need to be! 10%... yes, only 10%... that's enough to set you apart from the crowd, to get you noticed, to illustrate why you are more valuable than any of those other people that just "suited up and got ready to play" for the job.

Instead, you are here, suited up, and putting in 110% all the time to give you the edge, the added value to the company that presents you with that golden opportunity you have been searching for!

You know, when you stop to think about it, 10% really isn't that much more, it really isn't that tough to obtain, it really isn't that big of a sacrifice to give to land you the perfect career opportunity, to get you the one position that you've only been dreaming of.

10% is not reinventing the wheel, it's not even throwing out all you already know, no, indeed. 10% is just a little more, a bit higher level of commitment, just a little better than the average person that has come through that door. Not too hard? Then, get to it!

Commit and recommit to doing the 10% more. That's all it takes to be better than everyone else, to realize more of the pie for yourself, to get noticed and earn the favor of others.

Imagine, you are a waitress in a country themed restaurant. For you and your fellow co-workers, the music is the same, the atmosphere is the same, even the manager and the menus are the same.

Now, the question is "How can you get bigger tips?"

The answer is simple - by doing 10% more!

Yes, just 10% more than the other waitresses. That means you work a little faster, a little nicer, be a little more attentive to the customer needs, and ask them to come back to your section in the future. You may even wish to have them fill out a comment card or give them your business card, so they can remember to ask for you by name next time.

Remember, in business there is an old adage that says, "80% of your business comes from 20% of your clients." This illustrates the power of the reoccurring tips from the same clients and how important it is to please each and every client, thinking them to be or to soon become one of the 20%.

Given that you are 10% better than anyone else on the floor and that you provide better customer service, then chances are your tips and other compensation will *greatly* exceed that of the others.

Humm... only 10% effort? Can you do that? Can you be just 10% better than those around you?

It will then only be a matter of time until your opportunities increase, your rewards increase, and your personal satisfaction level increases!

Writing A Resume That

SIZZLES!

Resumes are not that difficult to write. In fact, most of us have probably created one at some point or another in our careers.

If you have, or even if you have not, you have probably NOT written a resume that SIZZLES!

A resume that SIZZLES is one that makes you stand out and thus, rises to the top of potential candidates. You can't be just like the other 12,000 resumes that your potential employer has received this month and expect to be deemed more important or a better candidate than any other just on the sheer merits of your layout or qualifications.

I am suggesting that you need to stand out but not so far as to use hot pink paper or write everything in some weird script font that only you and your computer have heard of.

Even companies that tell you they are looking for someone that can "think outside the box" are not looking for people that think all that far outside the box!

Resumes are intended to acquaint employers with you, your skills, background and education. Every resume will include work experiences, a listing of training and education, and the ever popular "References available upon request." statement.

But how do you make your resume really stand out from the hundreds of others? The quick, easy answer is that you sell your benefits, not your features.

As you prepare your own resume, you must first put yourself in the mindset of a marketer. You are your own product and you are selling "Product You" rather than a car or can of soup.

Nevertheless, the thinking is the same. Just as every car has a steering wheel, tires, and a comfortable seat so does every potential job candidate have a work history, educational history, and references.

You need to separate yourself from the crowd just as the automotive retailers do, one "takes you to the mountains", another sells cars for "unique individuals", the "soccer mom", or a "family on the go", while yet another has the best price or is located right in your neighborhood.

They sell the benefits of the product. This is what we call "the sizzle".

Think about it. Rather than just the features, they sell the benefits of automobile ownership, appeal to your ego, or encourage you to want the latest, the greatest, the fastest, the newest, the best.

Sell your sizzle!

What does that mean and how does that apply to my resume?

You sell your benefits to the company.

You seek to include words that emphasize your confidence and authority, for example. Then tell the reader that you managed, achieved, improved, directed, spearheaded, produced, trained, or created. The sentence would read, "I trained, managed, and improved call center personnel and their performance achieving a 115% gain overall in customer satisfaction."

Now, apply this to your own situation - pour on the sizzle - use those action powerverbs in your work experience, educational experience, and life experience portions of your resume.

Remember, your objective should also reflect a well defined and action oriented statement regarding the opportunity that you are seeking. For example, you are not just seeking an entry level job in the marketing department but "a challenging opportunity that benefits the organization by enhancing the company's image while utilizing my skills in managing, organizing, and presenting product information directly to the consumer to positively influence product purchase and long-term consumer buying habits."

Typically, your resume should be only a page in length and easy to review for the reader.

Utilizing bullets, whitespace, and other design considerations can also make your resume more desirable to read.

Usually a one inch margin on all four sides, double spacing between sections, and the avoidance of fancy artwork are recommended.

Be sure to proofread for spelling and grammar mistakes that your spell-check missed.

Most people stick with the white, ivory, or gray papers in a slightly heavier weight than most copy paper.

Artwork and cutise flourishes should be avoided in most cases.

One of the questions that I am asked the most is "What about salary or wages? Should I put anything on my resume about money?"

I generally suggest putting 'negotiable', 'open', or 'anticipated salary within industry norms'. This allows for some honest negotiation within the interview and candidate selection process. How do you become aware of the industry norms? Research Labor Market Information (LMI) compiled by the federal and state government based on surveys of businesses with the same positions in the same industry. There are national pay ranges, then regional, state, and regions within the state providing a given pay range for each particular job.

Another large consideration that many candidates don't spend enough time on is the face to face presentation during the interview. If you walk in unsure, without clear goals and direction, and without the confidence that you are a worthy and viable candidate for the position, then chances are you will be passed over for a candidate that appears much more positive, self confident, and enthusiastic, given identical resumes.

Employers view all candidates as trainable but bad attitudes and low self esteem can leave you out of the running very quickly.

The actual layout of the resume is always a personal choice but I usually suggest the typical block style.

Centered at the top of the page will be your name, address, and phone number(s) with either just your name or you may choose the entire thing in bold type.

The first section is entitled: Objective. This objective is written from a benefits frame of mind rather than the me-me-me writing that most are presented in.

The second sections is either Work Experience or Education, depending upon which area is your strong suit. Again, the powerverbs are utilized in short paragraphs describing actual courses or functions of the job you were in and how this may benefit your potential employer.

The third section is the opposite of section two. In other words, if you used Work Experience for section two, then section three will be Education. But, if you chose Education for section two, then section three will be Work Experience.

The fourth section I call: Life Experiences. This allows for much more information than the usual hobbies or awards and achievements sections.

I choose Life Experiences so that I may include my volunteering, my awards, my hobbies, and my big life altering experiences like traveling to Paris. These types of references are important and valuable to the potential employer because they come to realize that you have had experiences beyond the norm that may be beneficial to them.

For instance, in traveling to Paris, you had to deal with customs, language changes, cultural changes, hotels, airlines, reservations, luggage, transfers, tourism, and more. Therefore, if they were opening an office in another location, say another country, your skills and experiences with these types of issues may be quite valuable for the company. You may well be the candidate they select to send to just such an assignment with, of course, a bonus and substantial pay increase. ☺

If you had any military experience, I would include this in the section with my Work Experiences.

The entire resume would close with "References available upon request." centered across the bottom.

Again, one page should be enough for most people, two at the most. Any more than that and you had better be applying for the position of CEO or something of that sort which would typically require many more pages to extol your benefits and virtues.

You may choose to create your resume yourself or you may enlist my custom resume writing services by contacting me directly at:

Eddie Powell, PO Box 65, Reynoldsburg, Ohio 43068-0065

Eddie@EddiePowell.com

GETTING THE APPOINTMENT

(Your Cover Letter)

Getting the appointment is the sole purpose of the cover letter. In a marketer's perspective, this is the sales tool that gets you through the door and gets you face to face with the potential client - your potential employer.

Good, well written cover letters are as hard to find as good, well written sales letters that come to you in the mail trying to get you to buy everything from replacement windows to bottled water.

It is always worthwhile to study others work and see if there are any facets of it that would or could translate to your use and purpose.

You will notice after some study that all of these

letters have

some things in common:

They have an **opening** - this is the attention getter;

a **middle body** - this explains the offer and really does the selling;

and a **close** - this is the call to action stating that it's a limited time offer, when the discount runs out, or some similar hurry, hurry, do it now kind of pitch.

The same will be true of your cover letter. You should have an open, a middle body, and a close.

The entire tone and verbiage is very important. You want to relate well to the potential employer while not coming across too confident that you appear ego centered or overconfident. You also want to respect yourself and the reader, bearing in mind that you are both professionals and you both are quite busy.

As far as the actual layout, I suggest consistency with your resume which should be attached in your package by placing your name, address, and phone number(s) centered in the top and bolded.

Then, return down two lines and put today's date against the lefthand margin.

Index down two more lines and include the full name with title, company name, address, and phone number of the person(s) you are mailing it to.

Index down two more lines and type your salutation, like "Dear Ms. Jones:" or "Dear Search Committee:" for example.

Index down two more lines and begin your opening.

You opening should grab their attention within the first two to three lines. Do not use something like, "I saw your advertisement in the local paper...."

Instead, acknowledge them with something like, "I have explored the industry and determined that I would welcome the opportunity to apply my skills in managing finances and directing people within your organization, the recognized market leader. Certainly, you must always remain active, attentive, and aggressive to maintain your leadership position and I thrive in environments of this type where I may best utilize my talents of creatively encouraging my fellow co-workers to produce higher than expected results on a consistent basis."

Notice the attention grabber and the benefits you bring to the table. This will be much more effective than the typical "I saw your ad in the paper...." type of cover letter that most human resource people receive day in and day out.

Next, you want to build on your benefits with the use of more powerverbs as you describe former experiences and opportunities that you have harnessed to the benefit of past employers. Include some numbers like "I managed, directed, and implemented aggressive new procedures in the customer service and retention department that effectively brought our call center activity to new highs and accomplished an 83% retention rate, a full 17% better than the previous high."

See how this builds on the interest of the reader that you established in the open? You almost force them to read the body of the cover letter because they don't want to let the big fish get away (yes, that's you!)!

The body is not just a restatement of your resume. No, don't try just changing a few words around. It will be best if you talk of those experiences and how you can benefit your potential employer.

The close seals the deal. Remember, the objective of the cover letter is to establish an appointment. Recall, also, that the human resource director is busy and that the fastest way to encourage action (action being - the appointment) is to do their work for them, in the sense that you will call them.

Yes, you call them!

Establish a time and date in your letter. For instance, "I will call you Tuesday at 10:30am to establish a time when we could meet."

You've established the action. Now, follow through. Very important!

Call as promised and establish a time and date to meet with them to "discuss my talents and how I may best benefit your company."

If the recipient is available when you call, terrific! Establish a time and date in a very professional manner and get off the phone, thus, respecting their busy schedule.

If the recipient is NOT available when you call, then perhaps the secretary will have a message for you with a proposed time and date. If not, establish a future time when you can call back when your recipient is available to schedule an appointment, if the secretary cannot set an appointment.

Either way, this accomplishes your immediate goal, to get an appointment!

Now, get ready for the interview…

Interviewing

With

POWER!

Well, here it is! This is the moment you have worked so hard for. This is when they talk to you and you talk to them and try to come to the mutual understanding that you are the best person for the position.

But, if you are like a lot of people, this is where you choke!

This is where the tension starts building up inside and you may not even feel like getting out of bed to go to the interview.

Or, you could be the other type of person that we typically encounter. The super confident, perhaps overzealous type that believes that all they have to do is sit down and start talking and the interviewer will quickly realize just how lacking they have been without you.

Ideally, you will be somewhere in between. Confident but not overbearing. Ready to sell yourself but not to the point that no one else can get a word in edgewise.

It is important to relax and not let the stress of the situation overtake you to the point that you cannot think or express yourself well in the interview.

You should appear poised, confident, together, and fully able to discuss your strong points and weak points while presenting them in the best possible light. You should come across as capable but not to the point that your way is the only way to accomplish various tasks.

Be flexible and ready to learn new things.

Let the interviewer know that you have a certain level of experience and training but you are always ready and willing to learn new ways and try new things. They may suggest a short training program put on by the company or suggest that they will assist you with further schooling to obtain more knowledge or a higher ranking. Be ready to accept this and appreciate how it can make you a better employee that is more valuable to the company.

You may also express that you are willing to learn then teach the same material to others coming in the field behind you, as the company grows. This is a great way to be elevated to a supervisor or management level more quickly than those around you that do not provide similar opportunities for those newer employees just coming into the department.

Learning and teaching should become a natural part of your life, on and off the job.

Now, when we get down to where the rubber meets the road, the hardest part of doing an interview is having good answers for all those questions they ask, huh? Ideally, if you had the questions ahead of time, you could study and come up with terrific answers, right?

Well, here's what you have been waiting for...

The Tough Interview Questions

(and Their Answers)

Well, tell me about yourself. This is a question that most interviewers will ask early on. This is one of their favorite open-ended questions that allows you the opportunity to answer in a variety of different ways, but, be careful to not fall for their trap of telling all the negatives about yourself and very few positives! Instead, heavy up on the positives, the benefits you are uniquely offering this company, and why you would make a tremendous asset to the company.

What are your strengths and weaknesses? Most people can come up with a list of strengths that would be important to the position to which they are applying like caring, quality customer service, and focus on detail for a nursing related position. The weaknesses remain the questionable part. Think this through. Do they really need to know that you tend to blow up when confronted or you hate to do paperwork? I don't think those weaknesses will get you the position. Instead, offer up something like you tend to stay until the job is finished or sometimes you've been told that you care for your patients too much (again, nursing focus). These choices take weaknesses and turn them around into subtle strengths.

Do you think that academic grades are representative of most people? A couple of things to note with this sentence. First, "most people" is not who we are really talking about, truth is, we are talking about you. So, answer directly for you, not anyone else. Second, if your grades were good then use this opportunity to say so and even discuss your favorite subjects (the ones that pertain to the position you are going for). If your grades were not so good, then point out that your grades represent only where you were at that moment in time and since you have matured, experienced more, and grown a whole new cast of friends focused on new and different things, then you are not the same person as you were when your achievements were unfocused on this career. You have moved forward from where you were at that moment in time and are ready to earn and achieve much more!

On the job, how do you feel most rewarded? Some common answers mention money, awards, citations, gifts, and other recognition. The best answer you can give relates to the satisfaction you receive in your heart knowing that the job was done right, the smile you received from the satisfied customer, or the thanks you earned from the client directly. Your primary rewards are internal, heart related, not external, money related.

What are your goals, short term and long term, and how do you plan to achieve them? Short term goals range from now to about 5 years out while long term goals usually talk about 5, 10, or 20 years from now. In the short term an admirable goal would be to advance my career by focusing my time, talents, and energy with a company that appreciates and supports their employees as they seek to benefit the company with quality customer service, increased productivity, and to encourage the best in others. Long range goals could be to increase my knowledge and education, advance in responsibility on the job, and to become a more valuable employee to the company.

This addresses the areas of employee retention, encourages investment by the company to train you and promote you to greater levels of responsibility as you learn to lead and manage a team of employees in an atmosphere of cooperation and encouragement.

If you were doing the hiring, what qualities would you look for in an employee to fill this position? The obvious answer is all the qualities YOU have! But, to put them in words, use several powerverbs and words like leader, team player, manager, director, communicator, fairness, able to resolve conflicts, understanding, encouraging, and so forth.

Are you willing to travel? Are you willing to relocate? These are very open ended questions that require more information prior to giving a yes or no answer.

For instance, travel to a fast food restaurant may mean across town, while travel to a computer program re-seller may mean a route in 5 states. The same can be true with relocating. One firm may mean to another city while another firm may mean to another country! Don't answer too quickly. Instead, suggest that you may be open to consideration but you would need many more details. These details might include whether they will buy you a house, move your belongings, are promoting you with the move, are increasing your salary because you travel and pay you mileage, etc.

Are you willing to submit to a probationary period?
This, too, is undefined and requires more information to make a qualified answer. Consider the length of time, whether this time includes training, will you be compensated adequately during this period, will your

pay increase at the end of the time period, and what requirements must you meet during and after this period. If all of this is something that you can live with or negotiate, then, consider it. Otherwise, this might not be the position or company for you.

What did you do on your last vacation? What did you do last weekend? These and similar questions are meant to find out if you are a living, breathing, human being with interests, things you enjoy, causes you care about, a life! The obvious wrong answer is anything similar to staying home, eating popcorn, and watching t.v. instead of going out and doing things, devoting some time to your favorite cause - could be world hunger or your children, or visiting friends and family for a change (and time to download). Watching too much t.v., knowing too much movie trivia, and spending too much time at home suggests that you are not a well rounded, active, involved individual that participates in your world, your community, or your family.

We are offering $X.xx dollars, is that O.K.? You should enter any interview or negotiation with a well defined dollar figure that you want to obtain (both in dollars per hour and yearly dollars) so that you can decide whether their offer is adequate for your needs and lifestyle. Obviously, the offers are related to what other similar employers are paying for similar occupations in the same geographic area. You can do your homework and be well prepared by gathering information from the Occupational Handbook available in most libraries. This will give you a salary range for the country while the individual state handbooks will give you information specific to regions and states. Know this number and you will be much more prepared coming through the door for the offer that should be made and in negotiating what you realistically should expect for your occupational choice.

An important note:

<u>Be sure to listen to what is NOT said as well as what IS said.</u> For example, say you were applying to be a school bus driver and the interviewer said you would be working 8 hours a day and you automatically assumed that they meant 8 consecutive hours a day. Perhaps the interviewer really meant 4 hours in the morning to pick up students, a few hours off during midday, then 4 more hours in the afternoon to return the students to their homes. Now, the midday off period of time may be welcome and quite acceptable to you, but, if it was unexpected and not made clear,

then you may feel a little betrayed when really it was a lack of communication from both parties involved.

This not only applies to hours, but benefits, travel, promotions, working conditions, shift, location(s), union vs. non-union, and much more. Just be aware and don't get caught. Your assumption(s) can cost you a lot of money, time, and reputation.

At the end of the interview, they'll always ask:

Do you have any questions for me? Say "no" and you just struck out! Instead, come to the interview prepared with 6 or 8 questions. Questions like those issues you are now aware of but did not hear voiced during the interview. [See above section: <u>Be sure to</u> <u>listen to what is NOT said as well as what IS said.</u>]

-

You could certainly ask questions of them relating to promotions from within, personality testing, turnover, standings within their industry, their competition, their strategic plan, their mission statement, and any new divisions or ventures that they are entering or exploring at this time. You may have questions on holidays, forced overtime, unions, vacations, company buyout, their short term and long range plans, their involvement in the community, if they provide paid time to assist in the community, and so forth.

The Number One best question that I like to ask the interviewer is also open ended and can provide some valuable insight and quite an education about the company's actions. It is:

"How long have you been with the company and tell me about the experiences you have had with this company?"

Again, open ended and quite possible to provide some very interesting insight into the thinking and inner workings of the company. Be ready to respond and perhaps, even delve deeper into the answer provided. Could be fun!

Need some more help with those questions, what to say, and how to say it?

Simply email Eddie@EddiePowell.com for more suggestions. Remember, this exchange, their questions to you and your questions to them, is the real "dance" of helping each other feel comfortable with the other party quickly. Many opinions are crafted and decisions made based on the answer to these several questions. It is key to become calm, cool, and confident when delivering these answers and your follow-up questions to win the position.

Ways to Blow The Interview

(The Things You Want To Avoid)

There are a number of ways a prospective employee can blow the interview.

A quite common problem is the choice of attire or lack of it. Typically, your choice should lean towards conservative attire and a business, professional look. Suits are great for both men and women.

Remember to tone down the use of color utilizing more of the dark blues, browns, blacks, and greens rather than the reds, oranges, yellows, and such. In most cases, body piercing, tattoos, and jewelry in excess is discouraged. So, too, are all the scents, smells, and overuse of make-up.

Obviously, issues of hygiene, cleanliness, and personal care can affect the interviewers perception of the prospective employee.

Your personal choice of vocabulary - street language versus business language - for example, will have an effect on how well you relate and communicate your thoughts to the interviewer.

Remember, it is not the big words you use, but the proper use and effective communication you perform with the words and messages you do choose.

As you portray yourself, your goals, and objectives to the interviewer you can easily blow the interview.

For instance, being too focused on the money and not the career choice can lose it for you.

In turn, being too focused on training and educational opportunities can give the idea that you are just here for the training, then you are planning on moving on down the road to a competitor that may pay a dime or two more.

When asked what job they want in the company and replying the President's job, sometimes can make the interviewer perceive that you want too much too fast.

Remember not to tell any dirty jokes, make reference to all the guys that went partying with you last Friday evening, nor the amount of beer you can drink at one sitting. Dignity, sobriety, and maturity are the issues of importance during the interview.

The interviewer is trying to determine whether you can work with people of the same and other gender, other cultures, other religious backgrounds, individuals of differing sexual lifestyles, and people that have experienced life from a different point of view from yours without creating some kind of havoc and discontent in the workplace.

Know that they are looking for people that can make decisions that bring a level of maturity with them, and that enjoy new experiences, new cultures, and learning new things.

They focus on how well you can express yourself, how well you operate under pressure (like in the interview situation), the type of environment you like best (indoor / outdoor; well lit / darker; hot / cold; air / underwater; etc.), and how well you can complete forms (like their application).

They are expecting you to be prepared with several copies of your printed resume, a printed sheet of references, and all documentation that may be needed to obtain the position you are seeking (drivers license, diploma, certificates, medical records, social security card or green card, and more).

Quite frankly, they are asking themselves, do you "fit" the position and the company's cultural atmosphere?

Can you work here and be successful, thus, benefiting the company's long range plans and goals? Are you worth the investment in time, money, and energy to bring on board and integrate into the company? Are you the quality of person that the rest of our employees would work well with? Can you be trusted?

ARE YOU ONE OF US?

That is the ultimate question. Do you walk like a duck, talk like a duck, think like a duck, act like a duck? Then, you must be a duck! Therefore, since we are all ducks and so are you... welcome to the land of ducks!

But remember, if you are a peacock, simply trying to "fit" in the world of ducks, you will be found out! Yes, you may be able to adjust and thus, "fit in". Others that cannot adjust will be bypassed initially or perhaps, let go at a later time. This is not all bad.

To be happiest and most productive at your career you and your company must "fit" each other. So, if you choose a company and then get overlooked, remember, the interviewer is on the inside and it is their job to decide whether or not prospective employees really "fit" the company.

You may assume you "fit" looking from the outside in. But, the interviewer may know more since they are looking from the inside out. Don't dwell on being disappointed, instead, go on down the street where you will be appreciated - a better "fit"!

Finding more with Follow-Up

Follow-up is similar to the follow-thru of a baseball player or a golfer. If the swing action was stopped only half way rather than following thru, it is no telling how many balls would be lost and championships given to other players. The follow thru is what really sends the ball sailing.

The same is true in the employment search.

The follow-up is critical to your long term success. It is really quite simple to do.

Just take a moment on your way home from the interview to mail a Thank You note (yes, buy the pre-printed ones at a card shop) thanking them for taking their time to speak with you. Not only will this set you apart from the crowd but will keep you on the top of their mind should another position become available within their organization. Truth is, they may even phone you to let you know about something that might be quite suited to you at another division or company!

Everyone likes to be appreciated and so few of us really feel that we are. Just taking the moment to say Thanks will be remembered for quite a while.

You may even choose to stay in contact with that person for a long time as you seek to expand and move up within your chosen career field.

It's hard to tell what position may open up a year or two down the road within that company that the interviewer may recognize would be the right "fit" for you, since you do have more training, more experience, and you have stayed in touch.

Really, keep them informed of your moves and accomplishments... the results could surprise you!

Keeping Your Dream Job

What are the problems every company deals with on a daily basis? Things like providing quality customer service, making a profit, retaining good employees, providing an atmosphere that people want to work in, keeping costs down, getting more clients, and so forth.

You want to keep (or for that matter, get) your dream job?

Then, solve one or more of the above mentioned "problems". It really is that simple!

Put yourself in the mindset of helping the owner / the company achieve those goals – solve those problems – and you will have your dream job for as long as you'd like to have it. Seriously!

No one likes to work harder, longer, or without any help. Help the company achieve more with less, assist more people, increase profits, cut costs, and provide quality customer service, and you will be their hero, their fair-haired child, their star employee!

This is how you become valuable and stay valuable to the company. Focus on solving one or more of their problems, do it with skill and determination, and you will be on their team for a long, long time. Be able to convey your thoughts on how to accomplish this in the interview and on the cover letter. Relate to their issues and problems, not yours.

So, keep you eye on the ball - the owner / company perspective - and you'll be a

WINNER!

SOCIAL MEDIA

Taking The World By Storm

At last count, Facebook had more members than... well, let's put it this way, if Facebook was a country, it would be number three in the world – as of this writing, but remember, more and more people are joining the world of Internet every day. This means that all of the social media networks are continually adding members daily.

While Facebook is the leader for the moment, Google Plus, LinkedIn, Yahoo, MySpace, and many others are still operating, offering new and different applications, and trying to become the next Number One. Add in Amazon, iTunes, the App stores, the gaming sites, YouTube, the other video sites, educational sites, business sites, magazine sites, themed sites including dating, weight loss, relationships, jobs, online radio and television, and so many more... quickly you see the enormity of this thing called Social Media and the Internet!

As you are looking for jobs, there are several sites that you should be aware of as you perform your job search. Including, but certainly not limited to, www.Monster.com, www.Ladders.com, www.FlipDog.com, www.DogPile.com, www.CareerBuilder.com, www.CollegeBoard.com, www.Dice.com, even your local State operated job posting site usually linked from your State Job and Family Services site or designated WIA (Workforce Investment Act Administrator) for your state. As an example, in Ohio this site is www.OhioMeansJobs.com and is run on a similar platform to www.Monster.com. Simple do a Google search for Job Posting Websites and you will quickly come to realize the huge numbers of sites and job postings. It almost seems overwhelming.

You may choose to do your job search by spending hours and visiting each and every site to try to locate your next job, submit hundreds or thousands of copies of your resume, write multiple cover letters, click "submit" over and over as you clock hour after hour... OR... you can utilize www.Indeed.com, search your ideal job in the search bar and identify the geographic area, then sit back and let the site spider crawl all over the web and aggregate the results into one long list of opportunities right there in front of you. Now, this does not pull in each and every listing, it does pull from the top 125 sites or so and compile a nice list that you may browse until your heart is content. Highly recommended: www.Indeed.com. Trust me on this and save an immense amount of time!

Additionally, many of the trade associations, industry specific, and government entities including state, county, township, cities, and other divisions operate their own websites which may or may not feature job postings of interest to you. The Federal Government is the world's largest employer and offers many jobs, grants, and opportunities across several different websites (wondering which ones? Do a google search to find them all).

Note: You may hear of government job cuts, hiring freezes, and so forth. While these may be well intentioned, the truth is that the government is like a world unto itself operating within the outside world as we know it. To illustrate this, if the state needs a medical doctor within the corrections system, you can bet the job is posted and the recruitment efforts are underway. Same would go for other essential needs including nurses, guards, firefighters, security, and others in a variety of worksites and pay scales.

Facebook is so popular that the United States Department of Labor (the government agency that deals with jobs) now has a Facebook site. Other government entities are also following suit, so utilize your Facebook search bar, enter "jobs" or "job postings" and you are sure to find another source of opportunities.

www.LinkedIn.com offers a number of job postings while allowing others to search your profile for specific key words that may be appropriate for a specific job posting they are offering. This allows for a match-up that can be instituted by the company posting, a head hunter, or the job seeker searching for the job. What a nice surprise it is to receive an email from someone stating that your profile matched their search and you would you please consider applying for their identified position! Nice…

There are a number of sites that you can create your own 'bot, that is, a robot that goes forth on the Internet searching for job matches for you, retrieves them, and compiles your own customized list of job opportunities for your review as determined by your selected inputs. This, too, is a real time saver during your job search.

Remember, too, that there are still some employers that take the stance that they would rather have a candidate that wants to work specifically for them rather than a candidate searching for anyone with a job opportunity in a specific field. Say for instance, the electric company would rather have a person that wants to work at the electric company rather than a person that has computer skills matching a particular position. They would seek to post their job openings only on their company website rather than any of the major sites allowing for a fishing expedition for someone that knows the job skills and duties. So, target your employer candidates well and continue to take a few moments to search their company job postings.

Don't forget to check with your friends on all of your social media sites to see what they are aware of and who they know that could help you get an interview for opportunities that you may be interested in. The way to think of it is this, most people know 125 people or more when you tally in grandma, former classmates, their local insurance people, hair stylist, and grocery store clerk. By letting this circle of friends know of your job search, you then tap into the 125+ people that each one of them know... from that second circle or even the third circle of their friends... is probably where your next career opportunity is hiding. Be bold. Tell others of your job search, the type of career you would like, location, and other key elements, then, get ready for your next career move is more than likely coming from within those three circles!

Web Portfolio's

First, let's discuss what a portfolio is in relation to your job search efforts. Your portfolio is where you gather all of your important documents, awards, positive write-up's, commendations, newspaper articles, letters of thanks from customers, favorable personnel reviews, training certificates, educational documentation, civic participation, church involvement, and other supporting materials that serve to evidence your growth and positive outcomes for a potential employer to see. In old school days, this was a large leather carrying case that would hold everything from a resume and cover letter to documents, awards, and other supporting material about you.

Many times items would be too bulky to fit in the portfolio, personal information could have been disclosed, items could get bent, crumpled, or otherwise defaced unintentionally. With the advent of technology, many of these items are much easier to store as scanned items, pictures, or other digital items. Combine them all together for the digital world in which we live and you have the makings of a professional portfolio that is easily transportable, accessible, and can be delivered promptly to the Human Resources request.

Now, combine these images, along with the PDF of your resume, cover letter, references, recommendations, and other portfolio items on the web or at the very least on your personal computer, in a folder for ease of emailing or posting to a job board. There are many electronic sites capable of hosting the Web Portfolio as you will find with a quick google search.

In many cases, the web portfolio site will allow for printed materials, pictures, audio, video, Ebooks, and so much more. Performing a few minutes of a mock interview on video and posting it to the site can give the real interviewer a great first impression of your verbal skills, grasp of vocabulary, and "fit" with the company culture.

Recognize that by setting a schedule and performing regular updates on your web portfolio or your personally located electronic portfolio, you can save a lot of time, trouble, and worry when the next opportunity comes to apply for the career move that gets you The Job You Have Always Dreamed Of ©.

Wisdom says, get current, stay current, and always be ready for the next opportunity or promotion that comes your way. Don't lose out to someone that is better prepared... ever!

Remember...

SUCCESS IS

INTENTIONAL!

Meet Eddie Powell

Eddie Powell is a Leading Authority on Workforce and Business Development and a Career – Business – Life Coach. His methods are customized for each client and each situation, not a cookie cutter format for the masses that does not take into consideration your purpose in life, goals, objectives and strategies, and methods of accomplishing what you believe you were put on this earth to do. He helps you realize what's holding you back, release and move forward with quantum leaps, then, provides additional learning and support through his positive attitude and purposeful living messages delivered through Eddie Powell's Power Thoughts texted to your mobile device or sent to your email. Get more information by emailing: Eddie@EddiePowell.com.

Eddie Powell is the host of the television show focused on jobs, careers, and hot opportunities in the marketplace called The Shared Resource Network Television Show. The weekly 30 minute program features different guests each week and provides valuable insight from some of the industries leaders. Having begun in 2004 and airing continuously each week since, this is one of the longer running programs available on television. Ask your local cable or broadcast outlet to carry The Shared Resource Network Television Show. The Shared Resource Network Television Show is a product of The Shared Resource Network, Inc.

Eddie is the President and operates CEAN – Community Employment Assistance Network – a networking organization focused on bringing together employers, education, government, agencies, career coaches, and job seekers to share resources, leads, information, and positive energy focused on helping others. The motto is: Together, we can do great things!

Eddie Powell is the 2007 U.S. Small Business Administration Journalist of the Year – Region V. He has also been recognized with inclusions in Who's Who In Entertainment, Who's Who In Business & Finance, Who's Who In America, and Who's Who In The World. He has been honored with Congressional and Presidential awards, worked on three important projects with the U.S. Department of Labor focusing on Workforce Development Issues, is included on several boards, and continues to focus on the synergy of careers, business, and life purpose.

Eddie Powell embraces knowledge, wisdom, and understanding. Ongoing, He strengthens himself in these areas through reading, lifelong learning, and studies into his faith and encourages others to do the same. He is a DBA Candidate in Business and Marketing, MBA-Marketing, BS-Business

Management, BS-Marketing, and holds a Doctor of Divinity along with a certification by the State of Ohio to perform weddings and other officiating.

Eddie Powell addresses many groups and organizations each year. His clients include small businesses, professional associations, schools, government agencies, churches, networking groups, corporations, and non-profits. He custom develops presentations and trainings specific to the needs of the group. Eddie is knowledgeable in a number of business and marketing areas. Typically, his presentations are quite interactive, thought provoking, and serve to bring his audience to a new awareness of the topic discussed and how it fits with the world around them.

He enjoys working with clients on financial performance, quality, productivity, customer satisfaction, employee satisfaction, retention, work + life balance, the changing workforce, discovering your life's purpose, critical thinking, strategy, moving your career and business to the next level, and other areas of interest. With a background in radio, television, podcasting, satellite broadcasting, writing and entertainment, he delivers presentations and seminars that are real-world, upbeat, and provide valuable information for his listeners.

To contact Eddie for further information about his books, Ebooks, recordings, and trainings, or to schedule him for a presentation, seminar, or personal coaching session, please write to:

Eddie Powell

The Shared Resource Network, Inc.

P.O. Box 65

Reynoldsburg, Ohio 43068-0065 USA

Eddie@EddiePowell.com

www.ingramcontent.com/pod-product-compliance
Lightning Source LLC
Chambersburg PA
CBHW070030210526
45170CB00012B/520